by Ellen Patrick
illustrated by James Williamson

Harcourt
SCHOOL PUBLISHERS

Copyright © by Harcourt, Inc.

All rights reserved. No part of this publication may be reproduced or transmitted in any form or by any means, electronic or mechanical, including photocopy, recording, or any information storage and retrieval system, without permission in writing from the publisher.

Requests for permission to make copies of any part of the work should be addressed to School Permissions and Copyrights, Harcourt, Inc., 6277 Sea Harbor Drive, Orlando, Florida 32887-6777. Fax: 407-345-2418.

HARCOURT and the Harcourt Logo are trademarks of Harcourt, Inc., registered in the United States of America and/or other jurisdictions.

Printed in China

ISBN 10: 0-15-358454-8
ISBN 13: 978-0-15-358454-1

Ordering Options
ISBN 10: 0-15-358357-6 (Grade K Above-Level Collection)
ISBN 13: 978-0-15-358357-5 (Grade K Above-Level Collection)
ISBN 10: 0-15-360690-8 (package of 5)
ISBN 13: 978-0-15-360690-8 (package of 5)

If you have received these materials as examination copies free of charge, Harcourt School Publishers retains title to the materials and they may not be resold. Resale of examination copies is strictly prohibited and is illegal.

Possession of this publication in print format does not entitle users to convert this publication, or any portion of it, into electronic format.

4 5 6 7 8 9 10 985 15 14 13 12 11 10 09 08

Six bugs come
out in the sun.
What will six bugs
do for fun?

Two of the six
go in a bud.
One will go and
sit in the mud.

Little red bug
can go down a well.
Little red bug
can give a big yell.

4

Two bugs mix up.
Two bugs get wet.
They do not want
to come out yet!

Six bugs zip, dip, and hop.
They look for fuzz at the top.

Six bugs come down on one big puff.

Six bugs are fed.
Six bugs go to bed!